TV TOYS

Anthony A. McGoldrick

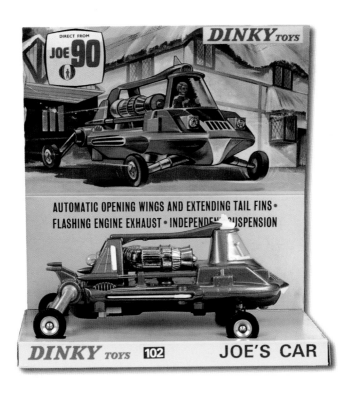

SHIRE PUBLICATIONS

Published in Great Britain in 2013 by Shire Publications
Ltd, Midland House, West Way, Botley, Oxford OX2 0PH,
United Kingdom.

43-01 21st Street, Suite 220B, Long Island City, NY
11101, USA.

E-mail: shire@shirebooks.co.uk   www.shirebooks.co.uk

A CIP catalogue record for this book is available from the
British Library.

Shire Library no. 723.   ISBN-13: 978 0 74781 217 3

Anthony A. McGoldrick has asserted his right under the
Copyright, Designs and Patents Act, 1988, to be identified
as the author of this book.

Designed by Tony Truscott Designs, Sussex, UK
and typeset in Perpetua and Gill Sans.

Printed in China through Worldprint Ltd.

13 14 15 16 17   10 9 8 7 6 5 4 3 2 1

COVER IMAGE
A selection of toys inspired by some of the most popular
television programmes of their time.

TITLE PAGE IMAGE
Dinky diecast model (102) of Joe's Car from the Gerry
Anderson series *Joe 90*. The car featured retractable wings
and had a battery that lit the rear engine compartment.

CONTENTS PAGE IMAGE
Left to right: The Saint's Volvo; Lady Penelope's
Rolls-Royce; The Green Hornet's Black Beauty;
Magic Roundabout car and Batman's Batmobile;
Supercar; Captain Scarlet's Spectrum Patrol Car;
The Man From U.N.C.L.E.'s Thrush-buster.

ACKNOWLEDGEMENTS
The author would like to thank all the people who have
assisted him in compiling this book, in particular Derek
and Linda Payne of Lothlorien Toy Museum in Moffat
for allowing him access to their collection; and also Tim
Newark and Russell Butcher of Shire Publications for their
efforts in checking the accuracy of the text and the quality
of the photographs. Louise Harker was of great assistance
in providing the images courtesy of Vectis Auctions. The
author would also like to thank his family and friends for
their support throughout the writing of this book.

PHOTOGRAPH ACKNOWLEDGEMENTS:
Alamy, page 5; By kind permission of Moffat Toy Museum
title page and pages 24 (top), 32, 35 (bottom), 38
(bottom), 42 (bottom), 44 (bottom) and 46 (bottom);
Copyright Vectis Auctions Ltd, pages 4, 8 (middle and
bottom), 10 (top), 11 (bottom), 14 (bottom), 16 (middle)
17, 18 (top), 21 (bottom), 24 (bottom), 27 (top), 28, 36,
38 (top), 39, 40 (both), 43 (top), 44 (top) and 45 (both).

CONTENTS

INTRODUCTION

T HIS BOOK is written for the collector of television toys. These days, wi
over a hundred television channels available twenty-four hours a da
there is plenty of scope for the collector. But in the early days television w
much more limited, with a choice of just a few channels, broadcasting fo
only part of the day.

In the early days of television, toy manufacturing was relatively difficul
There are examples of early bisque dolls with very ornate clothing, or met
prams, or carved wooden rocking horses and soldiers. Tin train sets an
lead-based vehicles were around from the turn of the twentieth century, b
good examples of these are rare, most often seen in museums. Raw materia
were hard to come by and during the two world wars resources such as woo
metal and fabric were used for the war effort, and not for luxuries such as toy
As television grew in popularity, so too did the manufacturing of toys
Thus, the toys from the earlier television programmes are rarer and ofte
more expensive. As toy production progressed through the 1970s and 80
cheaper materials were used and toys were often produced in vast number
with many of them being imported from the Far East. Many of these toys ar
less well made and consequently do not hold much financial value.

Some collectors may acquire TV toys related to a variety of programme
while others will specialise in one specific series or genre. There are collector
who are devotees of programmes such as *Star Trek* or *Doctor Wh*
and will collect nothing else, while others may have a collectio
related to cartoons, detective series, sci-fi, police programmes
or anything to do with Gerry Anderson.

Although television had its beginnings as far bac
as 1929, when the first broadcast was made, it di
not become popular until well after the end of th
Second World War. Strange as it may now seem, i
those days few people owned their own house o
had a car, and newly married couples would se
up home with 'hand-me-downs' from relatives.

An early boxed
stringed puppet
of Muffin the Mule
by Moko.

own a television set was the height of luxury. Children would play games
the street with a stick or a metal hoop, or would just be expected to use
ture as their playground. However, there was some public entertainment;
ople enjoyed going to the cinema and listening to the radio, and they
ad comics, books and newspapers. The characters in those media were
e forerunners of many of the TV toys, which nowadays have become a
ulti-million pound global industry.

After the war Britain began to settle back into peacetime life. BBC radio
roadcast more entertainment programmes than news bulletins, and people
ho were fortunate enough to see a television set would catch their first
ance of a programme dedicated to children. The programme was called
r the Children and was presented by Annette Mills. She played the piano,
alked to the children, and was accompanied by a 'friend' called Muffin the
1ule, who sat on the piano lid. The character was so popular that Muffin
1e Mule was given his own show, which ran on television until 1955.

Muffin the Mule became the first accredited toy to be related to a
elevision programme. Pelham Puppets produced a wooden version of Muffin.
nother company, Moko (later called Lesney, then Matchbox), produced
diecast figure of Muffin consisting of ten metal parts that were strung
ogether as a puppet. Boxed versions are rare and can command high prices.
Vhile this is a relatively expensive toy nowadays, it is also part of a highly
pecialised collectors' market, as are a number of early radio and television
ollectables. People tend to collect items that they can remember or relate to,
nd the earliest programmes were made over seventy years ago.

In 1949 *The Lone Ranger* was released as a television programme.
This black-and-white series featured Clayton Moore as the hero, with
Native American, Jay Silverheels, as Tonto. The show ran
'or several years and was very popular. The tradition of
cowboys and Indians as toys had been around for a long
time, but for the TV series toys were produced with
pictures of the stars on the packaging. Small plastic figures
were released by a well-known toy manufacturer, Crescent
Toys. These were generally unpainted and very affordable
for children. Toy pistols and rifles were manufactured by a
company called Lone Star and, while the unboxed versions
are still fairly common, it is difficult to find good examples
with their original boxes. Perhaps the most identifiable toys
relating to the *Lone Ranger* series were the dolls produced
by Louis Marx. They manufactured a range of figures,
including the leading characters, various villains, and even
the horses. These figures were about 12 inches tall and fully
articulated, with many accessories.

A carded doll of
the Lone Ranger
by Marx.

THE 1950s

IT WAS IN THE 1950s that television emerged as a popular entertainment. The biggest event of the 1950s for the British was the coronation of Queen Elizabeth II in 1953. The event was televised, and millions of people sought access to a television set in order to experience the celebrations. At that time, the BBC was the only channel broadcasting television in Britain. ITV did not start broadcasting until 1955, and then only on special television sets that could receive what were called Band III programmes. Television was strictly controlled, and programmes were shown only between 9 a.m. and 11 p.m. They were mainly factual, educational and sport; however, several programmes were devised for the entertainment of children.

As early as 1950, when most people were still listening to the radio rather than watching television, a programme called *Whirlygig* was shown featuring a character called Mr Turnip (see overleaf). Pelham Puppets, who were already producing Muffin the Mule, brought out a wooden stringed puppet of Mr Turnip, one of the first toys to be made in relation to a television programme.

Since the end of the war materials such as white metal and lead had again become available for toy making. Also, new tooling and techniques enabled toys to be produced and packaged in bright, attractive boxes – some of which are scarcer and so more collectable than the toy themselves, because the packaging was often thrown away while the child kept and played with the toy.

Closely following *Whirlygig* was a show called *Watch with Mother*, a television derivative of the radio programme *Listen with Mother*. The first *Watch with Mother* show was *Andy Pandy*, first shown as early as July 1950. Andy Pandy and his companions Ted and Looby Loo were very popular with children and featured in weekly comic strips as well as the black-and-white TV show. Comics had the advantage of colour, so toy manufacturers started producing brightly coloured toys, often using lead-based paint on metal figures. A company called Sacul produced beautifully made models of all three characters.

In 1952 Andy Pandy was joined by the Flowerpot Men on the *Watch with Mother* show. These characters were two animated figures who lived

Opposite:
Corgi No. 801 – Noddy and Big Ears, with Tubby Bear. The car also came with a Golly figure in the back seat.

in flowerpots at the bottom of the garden. Between them was a small flower called Little Weed. Again, Sacul produced a set of figures featuring these characters.

In 1955 Enid Blyton's 'Noddy' books were televised. *The Adventures of Noddy* was first shown on BBC, making Enid Blyton as famous in her day as J. K. Rowling is now. A great success, the 'Noddy' series featured several different characters, including Noddy himself, Big Ears, PC Plod, and a controversial Golly (who was the

Top: A lead figure of Mr Turnip from *Whirlygig*, made by Luntoy.

Middle: A set of lead *Watch with Mother* figures of Little Ted, Looby Loo and Andy Pandy, made by Sacul Toys.

Bottom: A set of lead figures of the characters from *The Flowerpot Men*: Bill and Ben with Little Weed, made by Sacul Toys.

aughty character). There followed a mass of toys relating to Noddy, including toy card figures by Corgi, puppets by Pelham, metal figures and vehicles by Budgie and Morestone. Of course, not all the toys were produced to coincide with the first showing. *The Adventures of Noddy* ran on BBC from 1955 until 1963 and was followed by *The Further Adventures of Noddy* between 1965 and 1973. Morestone produced the first Noddy car in 1956. The metal used in the early days of toy manufacturing is subject to fatigue, so many of these toys have suffered from damage. Morestone also produced an excellent figure of Big Ears on a bicycle, which incorporated moving parts (a rarity in those days). Big Ears's legs would go up and down with the pedals. Other toys by Morestone included a train set and a very rare boxed garage set. In the 1960s Corgi brought out three separate models of Noddy's car. They first produced a car (number 801) that had Noddy and Big Ears in the front seats and a Golly figure in the rear. The Golly figure was later replaced by a figure of Tubby Bear. There then followed a Noddy Car (804) that featured Noddy on his own. The show definitely marked a turning point for the manufacturers of television-related items.

ITV was launched in 1955 and one of its earliest shows was *The Adventures of Robin Hood*, produced by Sir Lew Grade. It featured Richard Greene as the lead character and ran for four years. The story followed the adventures of Robin and his men in Sherwood Forest, pitted against the Sheriff of Nottingham and King John. This show was aimed at older children and adults. The toy producers who capitalised on it were those who were producing figures of soldiers. Benbros Toys released a series of ten different painted metal hollow-cast figures, including a stag. Herald Figures brought out plastic sets of the main characters, and Kellogg's breakfast cereals featured a set of plastic

A rare boxed example of Corgi number 801, Noddy Car with Big Ears and Mr Tubby Bear.

A set of Benbros *Robin Hood* figures including Robin Hood, Little John, Friar Tuck, Maid Marion and others.

self-coloured *Robin Hood* figures as a promotion. Not all *Robin Hood* toys are related to the television series as the character has also been featured in several Hollywood films.

Another Hollywood adventure hero to feature on British television was Zorro. This Walt Disney series ran from 1957 until 1959 and starred Guy Williams in the lead role. The theme resembled *Robin Hood* in that the hero is a displaced nobleman fighting against injustice, but set in North America rather than Britain. Because of the American influence, some of the *Zorro* toys were produced in bigger numbers, and the Palitoy animated doll of Zorro is one of the most desired amongst TV collectors. Other toys relating to the series include plastic figures of Zorro on his horse by Lone Star, as well as more recent sets of figures by Gabriel. Another rarity amongst *Zorro* collectables is the *Zorro* sword and mask issued by Lone Star in the 1960s.

A rare boxed example of Zorro, the Masked Swordsman, by Palitoy.

Another children's series launched in 1957 was *The Adventures of Twizzle*. This unusual series is important for being the first production of Gerry Anderson, who went on to produce so many classic children's television shows. Twizzle and his friend Torchy the Battery Boy were characters loosely based on Pinocchio and Peter Pan. Twizzle was a living boy toy who escapes from a toy shop and ended up helping other toys to get mended. Gerry Anderson at this time was relatively unknown and worked with Reg Hill to try to improve the appearance of puppets on television. He later created a technique called Supermarionation, which featured cuts between animation and real people. There are relatively few *Twizzle* toys, but such items as records in colourful sleeves, annuals and card sets by Pepys are easily found.

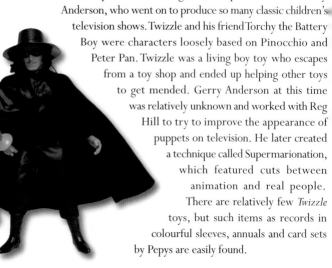

Another new television series released in 1957 was *The Pinky and Perky Show*. This was the creation of two Czech puppeteers, Jan and Viasta Dalibor. The show featured twin pigs, who were distinguished by the colour of their clothing. The show was initially aimed at young children but achieved a remarkable rate of popularity. *Pinky and Perky* ran for more than two hundred episodes. They released hit pop singles and albums, appeared as guests on chat shows, including the prestigious *Ed Sullivan Show*, sang with the Beatles, and featured famous human guests on their show, including Henry Cooper and Michael Aspel. The toys produced were mainly puppets, most notably by Pelham Puppets, who were now a market leader in producing boxed stringed creations.

A pair of *Pinky and Perky* stringed puppets by Pelham Toys.

The American influence was becoming more evident on British television and in 1957 there was a new western television series called *Wagon Train*. Still in black and white, it starred Ward Bond and Robert Horton as pioneers crossing America. It was a huge success in the United States, and many film stars made guest appearances. It was popular in the United Kingdom and ran for five years. The main television toys associated with *Wagon Train* are a diecast stagecoach manufactured by Budgie Toys and some board games.

Following on from the popularity of *Wagon Train* was another western series that caught the imagination of the British public. *Bonanza* was a story about a rancher in Nevada called Ben Cartwright (played by Lorne Greene) and his three sons, Adam, Hoss and Little Joe. The show was a great success and had over four hundred episodes, each lasting an hour. There were no diecast vehicles made but a company called American Character produced large articulated dolls from the series. With huge developments in manufacturing processes, they were able to create fully working figures with numerous accessories. Figures were made of all the main characters, their horses, and even a wagon to the same scale. Each figure was packaged in a colourful box with great artwork featuring the actor as the character from the show.

A carded diecast model of *Wagon Train* by Budgie Toys.

SPECTRUM IS GREEN FOR...

CAPTAIN SCARLET

A *Pedigree* PRODUCT

THE 1960s

TELEVISION at the beginning of the 1960s continued many of the established shows from the 1950s such as *Noddy*, *Pinky and Perky*, *Wagon Train* and *Bonanza*. There were repeat showings of the *Watch with Mother* series as there was now a growing demand for programming as more and more people acquired a television set.

One of the first new programmes to be created in the 1960s was a puppet show called *Four Feather Falls*, based on cowboys from Kansas. The Four Feathers were magic feathers that were given to the lead character, Tex Tucker, by an Indian chief. Two of the feathers enabled Tex Tucker's guns to come to life and protect him from outlaws and baddies. The other two feathers allowed Tex's dog and horse to speak. This series lasted for only thirty-four episodes, but already it was showing the imagination and ingenuity of Gerry Anderson. The puppets were worked by strings but Anderson incorporated electronics to increase their realism. Toys from this programme are very rare and generally collectors can find only TV annuals or books.

Another new children's television show to hit the screen in 1960 was the American cartoon series *Yogi Bear and Friends*, created by Hanna-Barbera. This delightful series had developed from comic-book characters and was centred on the bears that lived in Jellystone Park and were looked after by Ranger Smith and Ranger Jones. Yogi had several companions, in particular his little friend Boo-Boo, and his girlfriend Cindy Bear. The characters were very popular and led to worldwide merchandising of toys. Louis Marx incorporated all the main characters into their Minikins series of small plastic figures. They also mass-produced some of the characters as ramp-walkers; these were plastic figures that would appear to walk if placed on a downward slope. Mebetoys of Italy released a diecast Yogi Bear car, which is very well made, but difficult to find. Pelham Puppets produced a few of the characters as stringed wooden puppets.

Animation was popular in the 1960s, and Hanna-Barbera continued their success with another cartoon series, *The Flintstones*, this time about a

Opposite:
A rare boxed doll of Captain Scarlet by Pedigree Dolls. The photograph shows the doll with the original pistol and holster, and with the plastic cap with drop-down microphone.

An Italian diecast model of Yogi Bear and Boo Boo's car by Mebetoys.

Stone Age family. The show centred around two families who lived in caves in Bedrock with their children and pet dinosaurs. The toys recreated this in both plastic and tinplate versions. Louis Marx produced a range of Flintstone toys that ranged from cheaper plastic ramp-walkers to much more expensive battery-operated dinosaurs. Fred Flintstone's tinplate car was called 'Fred Fluvver'. These battery-operated toys are very expensive nowadays as their production concentrated on quantity rather than quality. Lithograph tinplate toys are easily scratched and damaged, so do not survive in large numbers

A motorised model of Fred Flintstone riding on the back of Dino, by Marx Toys.

Marx also produced a variety of playsets, such as the Bedrock Express set, which included plastic figures. Marx toys incorporated a mixture of materials such as a combination of tinplate, plastic and fabric.

Two television shows released in 1961 proved to be milestones for the collector of TV toys. Gerry Anderson followed the tentative success of *Twizzle* and *Four Feather Falls* with another puppet-based show, which centred around a professor who produced a flying car called 'Supercar'. The show had a limited number of characters but became a huge success. *Supercar* toys are among the TV toys most sought-after by collectors. Pelham Puppets produced wooden puppets of Professor Popkiss, Mike Mercury, Jimmy Gibson and Doctor Beaker. The other character from the show was Mitch the Monkey. A very collectable set includes plastic figures of all the characters along with a plastic Supercar, manufactured by Cecil Coleman Toys. Possibly the best-known Supercar model is the Budgie diecast toy. These models are very vulnerable to damage, with the wings being easily scratched and the nose aerial often being lost. Fairylite, who specialised in plastic models, produced a larger friction toy of Supercar that is highly collectable. Remco manufactured a great Supercar toy that could be moved in different directions by inserting plastic discs.

The Avengers, launched in 1961, was a new type of show for Britain, combining fast cars and glamour with action and law enforcement. Starring Patrick Macnee as John Steed, the show ran throughout the 1960s, and as its success grew so did its budget. Initially there were a lot of outdoor scenes, as they were much cheaper to shoot than those using expensive studio lighting

A boxed version of Budgie Toys' model (272) of Supercar, complete with the original catalogue leaflet.

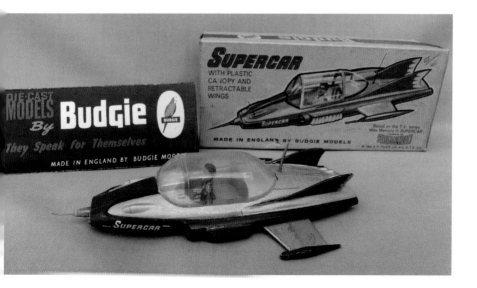

and sets. Patrick Macnee was joined in each series of *The Avengers* by a glamorous and feisty female assistant – Honor Blackman, Diana Rigg, Linda Thorson. The toys from *The Avengers* are centred round two main collectables. One is a very hard-to-find sword stick, issued by Lone Star. The stick itself is relatively unattractive as it looks like a walking stick that has a sword inside it, as used on the television show. What makes it collectable is the cardboard label featuring a picture of Patrick Macnee in his suit and bowler hat. The other main collectable from *The Avengers* is the Corgi gift set (number GS40) that includes Steed's red Bentley and the

white Lotus Elan sports car of Emma Peel (Diana Rigg). The gift set came with figures of Steed and Peel and three plastic umbrellas. The gift set sold well and the individual pieces are not hard to find, but the rarity lies in having a mint set complete with original

A rare Lone Star Sword Stick, based on the umbrella used by John Steed in *The Avengers*.

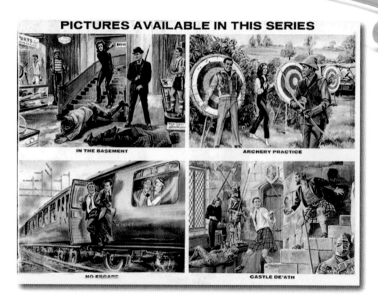

The back of an *Avengers* jigsaw puzzle by Arrow Jigsaws, showing all four pictures available in the series.

x, insert and umbrellas. Other *Avengers* memorabilia include the TV annuals ublished by World Distributors, as well as contemporary puzzles by rrow Jigsaws.

The following year more new programmes were being created for the owing ITV network. *Z Cars* was a BBC police series, launched in 1962, that ecame the forerunner of modern-day police dramas. Very little memorabilia as produced in relation to this series, but one item that collectors should ek out is the white police Ford Zephyr produced by Spot-On toys. It is oxed with an interior diorama showing that it was an official *Z Cars* item. here is also a large battery-operated plastic *Z Cars* police car released by alitoy which actually speaks when the blue light on the roof is pressed.

Many new programmes were being created for the growing ITV network 1962. Gerry Anderson continued his creative success with a futuristic uppet show called *Fireball XL5*. In 1962 space travel was still science fiction. nderson built a long rocket ship called Fireball XL5, staffed by an eclectic rew comprising Colonel Steve Zodiac, Doctor Venus, Professor Matthew latic, a robotic pilot called Robert, and an alien monkey called Zoonie he Lazoon. The show ran for thirty-nine episodes and was a huge success Britain, and later on syndication in the United States. The American uccess helped with the production of toys as it vastly opened up the market. *ireball* collectables include stringed wooden puppets manufactured by elham Puppets and plastic puppets by Cecil Coleman. There was a model f the spaceship, produced by the Italian company Quercerti, which was esigned to be thrown in the air and to float gently back o the ground on a parachute. There was a variety of lastic playsets manufactured by the American ompany MPC (Multiple Products Corporation). hese included larger sets such as Space City of *Fireball XL5*' and smaller set called 'Galaxy Patrol'. Each set had a ariety of ships, vehicles nd figures. Rare items nclude a friction plastic Jetmobile by Fairylite with figure of Steve Zodiac, and n even rarer Jetmobile by Golden Gate with figures of Steve Zodiac and Zooney. Other toys include space pistols, snow globes, jigsaws, card sets and model kits

A Palitoy plastic model of the talking police car from *Z Cars*. This toy was battery operated and had a small plastic record inside that played phrases such as 'Calling all cars'.

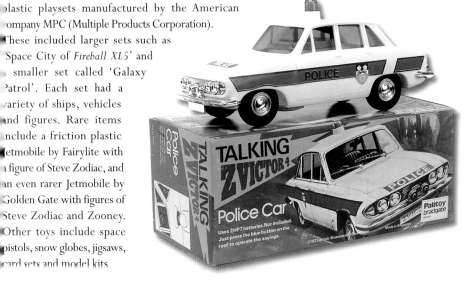

A rare Fairylite Jetmobile from *Fireball XL5*, complete with Steve Zodiac figure.

A Corgi model (258) of the Saint's Volvo, as driven in the TV series by Roger Moore.

Another big television show to debut in 1962 was *The Saint*, starring Roger Moore as Simon Templar, and comprising hour-long episodes about a reformed thief who had become an international playboy helping out people in need of his unique services. He was smartly dressed and drove a white Volvo with a personalised number plate, ST1. Despite the huge popularity of the series, it did not lend itself to much merchandising of collectables. However, a Corgi diecast car (number 201) was issued in two versions, one with a red bonnet label showing the Saint's logo, and a rarer version showing the bonnet logo in black. A later version of the car was released with Whizzwheels (renumbered as 258).

The first episode of *Doctor Who* was televised on BBC1 in November 1963. The programme is the longest-running British science fiction series and is syndicated throughout the world. Initially it was intended as an educational programme with the Doctor travelling to different places in time to illustrate history to children. The early episodes featured the Crusades, the Romans, the Aztecs and other historical characters, but all that changed when Terry Nation's Daleks appeared. *Doctor Who* caught the imagination of adults and children alike and was standard family viewing for several decades. The popularity of the programme was such that hundreds of different collectable toys were produced. The main manufacturers were Bell Toys, Codeg, Louis Marx, Palitoy, Berwick and Herts, though there were many more. The Daleks are among the most popular collectables, as well as some of the most expensive. Early Daleks such as the Codeg tinplate model are rare and generally sell for several hundred pounds. Louis Marx produced a range of Daleks in different sizes, some battery operated, others working by friction. The early Daleks are subject to damage such as rust and broken or missing arms. As *Doctor Who* continued in popularity, other toys were introduced such as the Denys Fisher range that included a Tardis, a K-9 robot dog, Leela (a female companion of the Doctor, then played by Tom Baker), a Cyberman and a giant robot. Items from the early 1960s are rare, examples being the Dalek Oracle game by Bell Toys, and the Berwick Dalek suit. Lincoln Toys produced two very collectable guns, the Anti Dalek Jet Immobiliser and the Dalek Neutron Exterminator.

A Marx boxed battery-operated Dalek from the *Doctor Who* TV series. The Dalek moved with 'mystery action' around table surfaces or hard floors.

A rare boxed
tinplate Dalek
manufactured by
Codeg Toys. The
black version is
the rarer colour;
the Dalek was also
available in blue.

Cherilea produced a range of 'Swappit' Daleks that were sold through Woolworths. These are very popular and came in a variety of colours with mix and match weapons. There was also a much rarer Cherilea Mechanoid produced around the same time. The Plastoid company brought out plastic badges of the Daleks and a much rarer version of the Zarbi (giant ants). *Doctor Who* collectables are currently being produced, with a range of figure and gift sets relating to all of the different incarnations of the Doctor.

By 1964 colour television was becoming the norm, especially for shows imported from the United States. *The Man from U.N.C.L.E.* was possibly inspired by the success of the James Bond films. Its two clean-cut heroes Napoleon Solo and Ilya Kuryakin, worked for an American law-enforcement agency called U.N.C.L.E., headed by Mr Waverley, which battled against communism and cold-war terrorism. As with most American shows, there was a wide variety of merchandise. Gilbert Toys brought out animated dolls of both heroes, and Multiple Toys issued attaché cases with guns, silencer sights and a variety of gadgets. Lone Star released plastic U.N.C.L.E. badges and Corgi produced two U.N.C.L.E. cars. The Corgi Junior car was the more accurate of the two as it was a model of a car that had actually appeared in the show. The better-selling model by Corgi was a diecast model of the 'Thrush-buster'. This blue Oldsmobile was released in a cardboard box with insert and packaged with a hologram ring.

In 1964 Gerry Anderson returned with a full-colour animated series called *Stingray*. This show was set underwater, rather than in space.

Corgi boxed model (497) of the Thrush-buster from *The Man from U.N.C.L.E.*

He committed to thirty-nine episodes of the show, featuring Troy Tempest as the captain of 'Stingray', Lieutenant George 'Phones' Sheridan as his co-pilot, and Marina, a beautiful mute aquatic humanoid. The theme of the show was an underwater battle with the evil Lord Titan, who operated a fleet of torpedo-firing Titan Fish craft. Lincoln Toys produced a plastic battery-operated model of the Stingray craft, and Lakeside Toys produced a tinplate friction version of the Titan Terror Fish. There was also a plastic friction version of Stingray by Lakeside Toys.

The following year Gerry Anderson produced his biggest yet animation production – *Thunderbirds*. This show would let Anderson combine all the techniques he had previously learned while working on *Supercar*, *Fireball XL5* and *Stingray*. *Thunderbirds* was based around the family of a wealthy retired astronaut, Jeff Tracy, who lived on an island somewhere in the Pacific. He had

A tinplate lithographed toy of the Titan Fish, made by Lakeside Toys. The Titan Fish was the enemy of Captain Troy Tempest in the Gerry Anderson *Stingray* series.

raised his sons to be astronauts and pilots, and each could fly one of the specially built Thunderbird craft. Scott piloted the Thunderbird 1 rocket; Virgil piloted the Thunderbird 2 transporter; Alan piloted the Thunderbird 3 rocket; Gordon piloted the underwater craft Thunderbird 4; and John was generally stationed in the Thunderbird 5 monitoring station in outer space. Jeff Tracy was helped on the technical side by an electronics genius called Brains. He was also assisted on land missions by Lady Penelope Creighton-Ward and her butler, Parker. Lady Penelope generally travelled in a pink Rolls Royce bearing the numberplate FAB 1, but she also had access to a power boat called FAB 2. The show was commissioned for only thirty-two episodes but each episode was an hour long. The programme was a toy manufacturer's dream, and all the main manufacturers wanted to produce items related to it. Pelham Puppets produced a series of wooden puppets, while Fairylite produced plastic animated dolls. Dinky obtained the licence for *Thunderbirds* and produced diecast vehicles of Thunderbird 2 and Lady Penelope's FAB 1 Rolls Royce. Gerry Anderson's success had allowed him to expand his production studio in Slough and to create a new company called Century 21 Toys, which brought out larger-scale plastic friction and battery-operated models of all the main Thunderbird ships as well as Lady Penelope's car. There are some variations within these models. Thunderbird 2 came with a red Jeep in the pod, but was also made with a model of the Mole digging machine. All of the early *Thunderbirds* toys are still highly collectable. The series was repeated many times on television, both in Britain and elsewhere. In 1992 there was a big *Thunderbirds* revival and manufacturers including Carlton, Matchbox and Pelham issued a new batch of toys on to the market.

Thunderbirds was a big hit with the toy manufacturers, but from January 1996 the toy industry enjoyed even greater success with the launch of *Batman*, starring Adam West and Burt Ward. This American series ran for 120 episodes

A Dinky
diecast model
(number 100) of
Lady Penelope's
FAB 1 Rolls Royce,
from the Gerry
Anderson series
Thunderbirds.
This model had a
front-firing rocket,
and harpoons that
fired from the back
of the car.

f twenty-five minutes and was widely syndicated around the world. The
now was based on a character already established in comics and consisted of
atman and Robin fighting a variety of dastardly characters such as the Joker,
he Penguin, the Riddler and others. Female characters were Catwoman and
atgirl. The toy industry around the world was producing dolls, cars, guns,
utfits, games, planes and costumes. Collectors can find toys from China,
apan, India, Mexico, Argentina, the United States and the United Kingdom.
Many of the foreign toys were unlicensed, mass-produced and often cheaply
made, but that does not deter the dedicated collector.

Some of the main collectables are the dolls produced by Mego. This
company produced dolls of all the major characters in a variety of sizes and
packaging, as well as a scale model of the Batmobile. Aurora produced a
election of model kits of Batman and Robin, and Cherilea made plastic
'Swappit'-type figures of the characters. Louis Marx manufactured miniature
Rolykin figures with ball-bearings in the base. In the United Kingdom Corgi
gained the licence for the diecast vehicles and produced a series of Batmobiles
over the years. They also produced versions of the Batboat and the Batcopter.
These were all available singly or as part of gift sets. Collectors try to obtain
a mint boxed version of each different packaging. The Batmobile underwent
several transformations and some of the variations were short-run trial
models that have become very expensive collectables. The wheels on the car
ranged from red wheels to Whizzwheels; while most models had black
wheels, there is also a version of the Batmobile with red wheels. The car
generally came with figures of Batman and Robin, but in the gift set the
Batman figure is in the car and the Robin figure in the Batboat. The packaging
was changed regularly. The first Batmobile came in a full cardboard box
with a cardboard inner piece. There was a 'secret instructions' compartment
under the box which contained plastic missiles for the Batmobile and a

Corgi Batmobile
(267). This highly
detailed model
contained figures
of Batman
and Robin and
featured a metal
chain-cutter at
the front, and
rear-firing rockets.

A boxed set of *Star Trek* communicators, made by Lone Star.

sheet of instructions. An unusual collector item associated with Batman is the gun. Batman never fired a gun in either the comics or the television series. However, that did not stop toy manufacturers such as Lincoln, Lone Star and Tada from producing an array of pistols, rifles and even a Batman Tommy gun.

While *Batman* was a huge hit both in the television ratings and with toy manufacturers, it was to be eclipsed later in 1966 when, in September, Gene Roddenberry produced a science-fiction series about the crew of the USS Enterprise called *Star Trek*. The original series consisted of fifty-nine episodes aired between 1966 and 1969, but it led to feature films and several spin-off series. The original crew comprised Captain Kirk (played by William Shatner), Lieutenant Spock (Leonard Nimoy), Doctor McCoy (DeForest Kelly), Lieutenant Scott (James Doohan) and Lieutenant Uhura (Nichelle Nichols). The idea was for the multi-national crew to travel through space in the future, experiencing many adventures. Again the show proved a hit with toy manufacturers. By now manufacturing techniques had advanced and all materials could be easily adapted. Toys were made from plastic, tinplate, resin, diecast metal, fabric and many other materials. Mego Toys produced a series of articulated figures of all the main crew members as well as several aliens encountered by them. The spaceships

A plastic *Star Trek* phaser manufactured by Remco Toys. The phaser had a sound effect and projected a light beam.

were manufactured as a model kit by several firms such as Revell, AMT and Aurora, and also as a diecast model by Dinky. The gadgets and equipment used by the crew in the series were also made into toys including phaser weapons, communicators, badges and full uniforms.

There were several other television shows produced during the mid-1960s that were exploited by the toy manufacturers. *Daktari*, released in 1966, was about a vet called Dr Tracy who ran an animal welfare sanctuary at Wameru in Africa, assisted by his nurse, Cheryl. The show featured a chimpanzee called Judy and a cross-eyed lion called Clarence. Corgi produced a green-striped Land Rover with plastic figures of the main characters (GS7), and a larger and very rare gift set (GS14) featuring the Land Rover, a giraffe truck (as used in Corgi's Chipperfield's circus range) and an elephant truck.

The Monkees were an American pop band of the 1960s who were created to rival the Beatles. They had several hits in the pop charts and went on to

Very rare Corgi Gift Set 14 from the *Daktari* TV series. The gift set included the *Daktari* Land Rover with figures, as well as a giraffe transporter and a Dodge elephant truck.

A plastic and tin model of the Monkee-mobile, made by ASC Toys of Japan. The Monkee-mobile was battery-operated and could play Monkees' music.

25

make a popular television show that ran for fifty-eight episodes between 196_ and 1968. Corgi Toys produced a detailed diecast model of their car in norma_ scale, as well as in a smaller scale called Corgi Junior. There is also a rar_ tinplate model of the Monkeemobile, which features a plastic record insid_ the mechanism.

The Green Hornet was a popular American series made by the same studi_ that produced *Batman*. The show was not as successful around the world a_ *Batman*, but was notable for being the television debut of Bruce Lee, who playe_ the part of Kato, the driver and bodyguard of newspaper tycoon Britt Rei_ (played by Van Williams). Kato was the designer of the gadgets used b_ the Green Hornet, and especially of his car, the Black Beauty, which wa_ manufactured in diecast form by Corgi Toys. There is also a large and rare_ tinplate version of the Black Beauty, made by Aoshin Toys of Japan.

A Man Called Ironside was an American series about a former chie_ detective of the San Francisco police. After being shot, he was confined t_

Boxed version of Corgi diecast model 268 of the Black Beauty from the TV series *The Green Hornet*. The car featured a front-firing rocket and a radar scanner that could be directed from the boot.

wheelchair but returned to work for the police, setting up a
specialised team of assistants. Played by Raymond Burr, Ironside was
driven around in a specially converted van to carry his wheelchair.
Husky Toys produced a model of the van that is easy to find on its
own, but much harder to obtain on its original card backing.

The Prisoner was a cult hit in 1967. The show starred Patrick
McGoohan as a secret agent who tried to resign from the service,
but was captured and drugged, and awakens in a mysterious coastal
village. This series had only seventeen episodes but intrigued viewers.
Dinky produced a single model of a Mini Moke from the series; this
is highly sought-after as long as it is original and has its distinctive 'taxi'
number plates and the striped canopy and rear wheel cover.

In September 1967 Gerry Anderson launched his latest animation
show, *Captain Scarlet and the Mysterons*, which was an immediate hit.
His reputation as an animator was now international and this new series was
a big money-spinner for Century 21 and ITC. The series involved a large cast
of characters; Captain Scarlet was an agent of Spectrum, and the Spectrum
personnel were all named after colours. There were futuristic-looking vehicles
for the land-based adventures, and a flying headquarters called Cloud Base
featured an airborne group called the Angels, who flew Interceptor jets.
Century 21 Toys brought out a range of larger-scale models, though they were

A carded Corgi
Junior model
(1007) of the van
used in *A Man
Called Ironside*. The
model featured a
working rear ramp
for the wheelchair.

Dinky Mini Moke
(106) from *The
Prisoner*. The car
featured as a taxi
in the actual series,
as seen on the
number plate

Angel Interceptor plastic kit manufactured by Airfix Toys. The plane featured in the Gerry Anderson series *Captain Scarlet*.

not all in proportion. Pedigree Dolls manufactured a 12-inch animated doll of Captain Scarlet (see page 12), which is among the most highly sought-after toys for TV collectors. The doll was a good likeness of Captain Scarlet portraying him in full uniform, including hat with visor, and with belt and pistol. Other collectables from *Captain Scarlet* include a 7-inch Pedigree figure of Destiny Angel and a bendy Captain Scarlet, as well as a Triang Magicars 21st Century Driving Set. Dinky Toys got the licence to produce diecast models of the vehicles while Airfix produced a model kit of the Angel Interceptor. The standard vehicles were the red Spectrum Patrol Car, the blue Spectrum Pursuit Vehicle and the white Maximum Security Vehicle.

In 1968 Gerry Anderson followed the success of his previous series by creating a show called *Joe 90*. Joe 90 is the nine-year-old nephew of Professor Ian MacLaine, who has invented a machine nicknamed the 'Big Rat'. The machine is capable of transferring brain waves from one person to another and the Professor perfects a process whereby the brain waves are transmitted into microchips in his nephew's spectacles. Thus Joe can think and act like anyone from a Russian pilot to a French scientist. He is put to work as an agent for WIN (World Intelligence Network) under the guidance of special agent Sam Loover. Joe 90 had some cool gadgets, which were manufactured by the toy makers. Pedigree Dolls produced an 8-inch figure of Joe in a red plastic suit. This doll came with the special glasses and a WIN badge and is very hard to find in boxed condition. In later years, toy manufacturers released *Joe 90* glasses and a briefcase containing some of Joe's gadgets. Waddington's produced a range of jigsaws and Dinky again got the licence for the diecast vehicles. They produced a very complicated model of Joe's Car (number 102 – see title page) and a sleek model of Sam's Car (number 108)

A Dinky model (103) of the Spectrum Patrol Car from the Gerry Anderson series *Captain Scarlet*. The car features a clockwork motor to give a 'realistic engine sound'.

A Dinky model (105) of the Maximum Security Vehicle as seen in *Captain Scarlet*. The model features opening gull-wing doors and a radioactive crate.

A Dinky Spectrum Pursuit Vehicle (104) as seen in Gerry Anderson's *Captain Scarlet and the Mysterons*. The vehicle was driven by Lieutenant Blue and features a forward-firing rocket, an opening side door with drop-down figure and rear caterpillar tracks.

Dinky models (108) of Sam's Car from the Gerry Anderson series *Joe 90*. The car featured a mechanised engine sound and is shown in maroon and chrome versions.

in three different colours: chrome, red, and a rarer pale blue version. Century 21 Toys produced larger-scale plastic models of both Joe 90 and Sam Loover's cars.

Another television series from 1968 was *The Herbs*, a short-lived animation series about an aristocrat called Sir Basil and his wife, Lady Rosemary. The stories take place in a garden and centre around Dill the dog and Parsley the lion. Dinky took up a licence from the BBC to manufacture a toy car with Parsley the lion as the driver. They used an already existing casting of a vintage Morris Oxford; other characters were included inside the box as cardboard cut-outs. There were also some glove puppets made

Boxed Dinky model (477) of Parsley's car from *The Herbs*. The box came with cardboard cut-out figures of other characters from the programme.

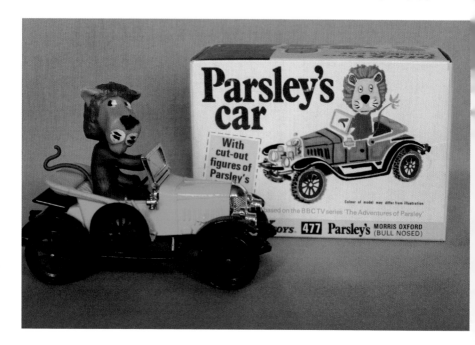

y Chad Valley and a Fuzzy Felts series of *The Herbs*. These particular toys
ppeal to the collectors of animated series but may be missed by some of
the more general TV toy collectors.

Gerry Anderson finished his successful 1960s sequence with an
xperimental show called *The Secret Service*, in which he was moving towards
ncorporating animation with real actors. His previous Supermarionation
echniques had involved cutting from animation to human hands but
he Secret Service went a stage further. His success allowed him to develop
hirteen episodes of the show, but it did not achieve the popularity of
upercar, *Stingray*, *Thunderbirds*, *Captain Scarlet* and *Joe 90* and ran only from
eptember to December in 1969. Stanley Unwin played an elderly clergyman
who worked as a secret agent for British Intelligence. He was codenamed
Bishop' (an acronym for 'British Intelligence Service Headquarters
Operation Priest'). Unwin's voice was heavily accented and he often spoke
n gobbledegook. Sir Lew Grade cancelled the show because it would not
yndicate internationally. However, Dinky Toys produced a model of Father
tanley Unwin's car, which was a modified version of a Model T Ford. The
oy sold well and is nicely presented in a cardboard box and insert format.

Thus, Gerry Anderson started the 1960s with *Four Feather Falls* and
losed the decade with a much changed format in *The Secret Service*.

Dinky model
(109) of Gabriel
from the Gerry
Anderson series
The Secret Service.

THE 1970s

B Y THE 1970s Britain had three television channels and the broadcasting hours had been extended, which led to a need for more programming. The 1970s was the decade of imported American shows. There had been several American series in the 1960s but television had grown up by the 70s; there were more outdoor locations and all the recordings were made in colour. The technology of television production had developed and competition was increasing across the various networks, so poorer-quality shows did not reach the screen. By the mid-1970s most people in the United Kingdom either owned or rented colour television sets.

Similarly, by the 1970s toys, too, were more complex and more mechanised; their boxes and packaging were more colourful and intricate. The basic diecast or pressed-steel cars of the 1950s and early 60s had been

Dinky model
(351) of the
UFO Interceptor.
This working
model featured
a forward-firing
missile.

Dinky model (352) of Ed Straker's futuristic car from the Gerry Anderson series *UFO*. The car came in gold, yellow or maroon.

eplaced by realistic cars, with engine sounds, opening doors and windows, nd detailed replica figures. The plastic figures had evolved from basic nimated types to much more articulated moulded plastic ones. In the 1970s he wooden stringed puppets and lead figures were displaced by fully jointed, lking plastic figures and very detailed, realistic accessories.

In the early 1970s there was a newly developed series by Gerry Anderson. Ie was moving away from animation but still had an intense love of uturistic-looking cars and spaceships. His new series was simply titled *UFO* nd was based around the concept of Britain having a military-style defence ystem against invasion from outer space. The defence organisation was called HADO and was secretly located beneath a film studio in southern England. t was headed by Commander Straker, played by Ed Bishop, who also acted s the head of the studio. The show was a deliberate move by Century 21 roductions to aim for a more adult audience and was a big success throughout he world. Anderson created twenty episodes, each designed to last a full hour. There was a large cast spread across three main locations: the studio, Moonbase, and an underwater craft called Skydiver. Again, Dinky obtained he licence to produce the diecast toys and initially released models of the green SHADO 1 U.F.O. Interceptor with its forward-firing missile and the and-based vehicle SHADO 2. They also produced a model of Straker's uturistic car, which was available in both yellow and gold.

In 1974 *Kojak* became a sensational hit on British television. It starred Telly Savalas as a New York detective who had the characteristic quirk of sucking a lollipop and whose catchphrase was 'Who loves ya, baby?' Corgi produced Kojak's Buick car (number 290), which was a basic brown Buick itted with a red police roof light and a separate figure of Kojak. The figure came in two varieties, the rarer being hatless. The colourful packaging featured a New York street scene and came with a plastic self-adhesive police lieutenant's badge. Corgi also released a smaller version of the car as a Corgi Junior model, as well as a twin pack featuring the car with a New York

Corgi model (290) of Kojak's Buick police car. The car was packaged in an attractive diorama box with a plastic police badge. Included was a plastic figure of Kojak, which can be found with or without a hat.

police helicopter. Lone Star also produce a boxed snub-nose cap pistol with Telly Savalas's image as Kojak.

Later in 1974 Lee Majors made h debut in *The Six Million Dollar Man*. The show was about Colonel Steve Austin, an American astronaut who had a near-fatal accident, but was saved by bionic surgery. With artificially enhanced legs, arms and eyes, he became an agent for OSI, run by Oscar Goldman. Majors was married to Farrah Fawcett and for a while they became Hollywood's golden couple. Kenner produced a series of articulated dolls, similar to Action Man dolls, of both Steve Austin and Oscar Goldman. Kenner also produced figures of the villains Maskatron and Big Foot, as well as accessory sets including Oscar Goldman's secret office, a repair station and a pair of bionic legs. The show ran on television for four years.

In 1975 Gerry Anderson returned to television with a futuristic programme called *Space 1999*. This was to be a sequel to his *UFO* series which had latterly featured several episodes set on Moonbase. The show starred Martin Landau and Barbara Bain, an American married couple who had previously appeared together in *Mission Impossible*. Sir Lew Grade wanted to capture the American market with this show. Other lead actors included Barry Morse as Professor Victor Bergman and, in the second series, Catherine Schell as Maya, a beautiful alien creature. The show was set on the moon, which had been knocked out of orbit by a huge explosion. The Moonbase was extensive and was fully staffed and equipped at the time of the explosion. It had spacecraft, including transporters and freighters. These vehicles were manufactured by Dinky Toys and became very collectable. The early version of the Transporter (359) came in green and were sold in cardboard boxes with clear acetate windows. The Freighter (360) came in metallic blue, though there is a much rarer version produced in white. All of the pods on these ships were interchangeable, so the pod from the white Freighter would fit the pod from the Transporter. Model kits of the spaceships were also produced by AMT and Airfix. The show's main characters were also produced in doll format; Palitoy manufactured a series of five dolls with realistic features, and originals of these dolls are highly collectable. Another set of three dolls was produced by Mattel, but these are less detailed and not so popular.

The following year *Starsky and Hutch* was released on British television screens, and it had plenty for the toy manufacturers to work with. The show

The back of the box for Kenner's *Six Million Dollar Man* doll. The picture shows the doll's features as well as other accessories available from Kenner Toys.

A boxed *Space 1999* stun gun, manufactured by Remco Toys.

had four main characters: Dave Starsky (Paul Michael Glaser), Ken Hutchinson (David Soul), Captain Dobey (Bernie Hamilton) and Huggy Bear (Antonio Fargas). Starsky and Hutch were two undercover cops working under Captain Dobey in Bay City in California. A prominent attraction was Starsky's car, a bright red Ford Gran Torino with a very distinctive white stripe running along the side.

Thus toy manufacturers had both a vehicle and figures to reproduce. Mego bought the rights for the dolls and released carded figures of the four main characters plus a baddie figure called 'Chopper'. Huggy Bear is probably the most collectable of the series, followed by Captain Dobey. The other figures sold in large quantities. The same figures were sold under licence in the United Kingdom by Palitoy, who also made a twin pack of *Starsky and Hutch* figures. The Ford Gran Torino car was produced by several manufacturers. Mego manufactured a car in the same scale as their figures; the boxed version of this is very hard to find in good condition. In the United States a large remote-controlled version was manufactured by Galoob. Corgi made the British version of the car, both as a basic Corgi Junior model and in a very attractive diorama box (model 292) with plastic figures of the two stars arresting a criminal. *Starsky and Hutch* was a great success and ran on television for four seasons, until 1979.

John Steed from *The Avengers* made a comeback in 1976. He was still a very dapper secret agent but he now had two new assistants: an ex-army major Mike Gambit (Gareth Hunt), and a beautiful and glamorous former ballet dancer, Purdey (Joanna Lumley). Now titled *The New Avengers*, the show was to run for twenty-six episodes, the last four being set in Canada. Steed was portrayed as a very wealthy man, and scenes filmed at his house showed the stables and a selection of expensive cars. The main vehicles used in the series were Steed's Jaguar and Range Rover, Mike Gambit's Range Rover and Purdey's MG sports car. Dinky obtained the original licence for the diecast models and immediately released a version of Purdey's sports car (113). The model used was a yellow Triumph TR7. Steed's Jaguar causes a lot of discussion within the TV toy collector's world. The car was advertised as Dinky model 112 and featured in the Dinky catalogues of the time. However, it never went into full production; about thirty-six official salesmen's samples were made of the car and these are extremely rare. Another popular collectable from *The New Avengers* is a rare doll of Purdey, made by Denys Fisher, which comes on a carded background. Purdey is dressed in a wrap-around skirt, which she wears over her leotard and leggings. Revell Models produced plastic construction kits of both Steed's Jaguar and Purdey's Triumph TR7.

Corgi model (292) of Starsky and Hutch's Ford Torino. The box came with a diorama insert as well as plastic figures of Starsky, Hutch and a generic villain.

In January 1977 a trio
¹ glamorous crime-fighters
.as launched on British
·levision. This was an
·merican series called
harlie's Angels and starred
.arrah Fawcett-Majors, Kate
.ackson and Jaclyn Smith as
aree lovely ladies recruited by
ne mysterious Charlie to act as
private crime-fighting agency,
nanaged by the inept Bosley
played by David Doyle). The
·eries was very succesful in
he United States and ran for
ive years, with 110 hour-long
pisodes. The three female stars
·nspired a rush of dolls from the toy
nanufacturers. Hasbro produced a
·umber of dolls and an extensive

A plastic
doll of Farrah
Fawcett-Majors as
Jill from *Charlie's
Angels.* The doll
was produced by
Hasbro Toys.

Dinky models from
The New Avengers.
Dinky model 112
of Purdey's TR7
was mass
produced but
model 113,
Steed's Jaguar,
never went
into production,
and only a few
salesmen's samples
exist.

ange of outfits in the United States. Later, Farrah Fawcett-Majors left the
how and was replaced by Cheryl Ladd, and Hasbro produced a doll of her
.s well. In Britain, the dolls were produced by Palitoy, and Corgi produced
. Chevrolet van (434) in *Charlie's Angels* livery. This was a standard model

Corgi model (342) of the Ford Capri from *The Professionals*. The car came in a diorama packaging with plastic figures of Bodie, Doyle and George Cowley.

from the Corgi range that w. simply painted pink and had suitab decals applied.

In December 1977 a new actic show premiered on British televisio. It featured the veteran actor Gordo Jackson as George Cowley, the hea of an elite anti-crime group calle *The Professionals*. The show general followed the adventures of the tw lead characters, Bodie (Lewis Collin: and Doyle (Martin Shaw), who wer expert in self-defence, weaponry an driving fast cars. It was the gun and cars that attracted the to manufacturers. The 1970s was th decade of fast Ford cars, particularl the Capri and the Escort, and these were the cars of choice for Bodie and Doyle Corgi bought the licence to produce the *Professionals'* Ford Capri (342). It wa packaged in a similar way to the *Kojak* and *Starsky and Hutch* models. The Ford Capri was released in silver with plastic figures of the three stars. A silve Capri was also released as a *Professionals* car in the Corgi Junior series, as wel as part of a twin pack, where it was paired with a Rover 3500 police car. Idea Toys produced a slot-car racing set that featured the silver Capri and a security van. Lone Star toys issued a toy automatic pistol and shoulder holster relate to the series, with colourful cardboard packaging. Thomas Salter Toys produce a *Professionals* Crime Buster Kit, which comprised a plastic gun, silencer telescopic sight, ammunition magazine, holster and shoulder support. The se also included a watch, camera, walkie-talkie set and CI5 identity cards.

In January 1978 the BBC launched a new science-fiction programme called *Blake's 7*. This show was to become a cult classic for sci-fi fans around the world. It starred Gareth Thomas as Roj Blake, the dissident commander of a spaceship called Liberator. At the time, the series had a big following, but there was very little merchandise, unlike American shows such as *Space 1999*. The main collectable released in the United Kingdom was a model of the Liberator spaceship made by Corgi Junior. The model was released in both white and silver and also came as a twin pack with a space shuttle model.

Corgi Juniors model showing the silver version of the spaceship Liberator from the BBC series *Blake's 7*.

Later in 1978 Bill Bixby starred in a new series from the United States. He played a scientist who has an accident

t work and, when angered, grows large, turns
reen and becomes the 'Incredible Hulk'.
he Hulk was played by champion bodybuilder
ou Ferrigno. Universal produced eighty-two
our-long episodes of the show. The Hulk was
popular character for TV toy manufacturers,
nd plastic models usually feature the big green
igure in torn purple shorts. Corgi Toys brought
ut a model of a Mazda pick-up truck with
he Hulk figure captured in a cage. This vehicle
ever featured in the show but was a popular TV
ollectable at the time.

In September 1978 a new British series
rought back the popular character of Simon
Templar in *Return of the Saint*. Roger Moore was
hen playing James Bond so the lead role was
aken this time by Ian Ogilvy. The producers
vanted a British car instead of the Volvo, and
Jaguar obliged by lending them the latest XJS
model, in white. The series was popular and the
car was reproduced by a number of toy manufacturers. Revell brought out
a model kit of the car, while Corgi Toys released not only a diecast model but
a larger plastic version, with a sonic control in the shape of a pistol. They
also produced a model Jaguar XJS in the Corgi Junior series.

In 1979 yet another American series was launched on British television
screens. This series centred around two brothers, Bo and Luke Duke,
who lived with their sister Daisy and uncle Jesse in the fictional county of
Hazzard. *The Dukes of Hazzard* was a combination of comedy and adventure.
The Duke boys drove a converted Dodge Charger car painted bright orange
and bearing the Confederate flag on its roof. The car, called 'General Lee',
was used to transport illegal moonshine around the country and almost every
week was involved in a chase with the sheriff of Hazzard and his police force.
The car was the star of the show and was produced as a toy by companies
including ERTL, Mego, AMT and MPC. ERTL produced an entire range of
cars from the series, including the police cars, a Cadillac, Daisy's Jeep and
a pick-up truck from Cooter's Garage. The diecast and steel cars were also
produced in scales ranging from Junior size to 1/18 scale. AMT and MPC
brought out plastic kits of the cars, and Mego not only released the main cars
('General Lee', police car and Daisy's Jeep) but produced carded plastic
articulated figures of all the main characters. The popularity of the show
was such that a mass of tie-in products was issued, including watches,
walkie-talkies and costumes, as well as the usual range of books, annuals and

A boxed Mego
doll of the
Incredible Hulk.

Corgi's plastic sonic-controlled model of the Saint's Jaguar XJS and the diecast version (Corgi 320) as featured in *Return of the Saint*, starring Ian Ogilvy.

trading cards. The series ran on television for six years, with 145 episodes being produced. Like several other popular television series, it was later adapted into a major Hollywood film.

By the end of the 1970s Britain was used to having colour television and a wide choice of programmes available. Black-and-white television sets were being replaced by newer models that came with bigger screens and remote controls. Video recorders were starting to become popular, allowing people the luxury of watching one programme and recording another, or letting the viewer record a programme to watch later. All this new technology meant that the programme producers had to supply more shows and were often starting to repeat older recordings. The British television channels were also beginning to purchase programmes from worldwide sources including foreign-language shows (which often needed subtitles) from Japan, France, Italy and elsewhere.

ERTL steel version of the Dodge Charger car from *The Dukes of Hazzard*. The car was known as 'General Lee'.

THE 1980s

TELEVISION went from strength to strength in the 1980s. Several of the television series from the 1970s continued into the 1980s, and during the decade *Doctor Who* was to become the longest running science-fiction series, continuing its run that had started in the early 1960s. The beauty of *Doctor Who*, from a producer's point of view, was that the main character remained the same even though he was played by different actors; during the 1980s Tom Baker, Peter Davison, Colin Baker and Sylvester McCoy all took the role. British television productions included many new game shows, comedy shows and quiz programmes during the 1980s, but they did not generate much to interest the TV collector. Again, it was the big shows from the United States that were of interest to the toy manufacturers.

In 1980 a classic science-fiction hero re-emerged in a new series. Buck Rogers had first appeared as a character in 1928 in a comic book called *Amazing Stories*, and in 1929 there was a comic strip called *Buck Rogers in the 25th Century*. In 1980 NBC brought their television series of *Buck Rogers* to Britain, starring Gil Gerard as the eponymous hero, with the beautiful ex-model Erin Gray as Colonel Wilma Deering. The series featured lots of aliens, spaceships, weaponry and a robot called Twiki. All of these were grist to the mill of the toy manufacturer. Corgi Toys produced a diecast model of Buck Rogers's Starfighter, complete with figures of Colonel Deering and Twiki, as well as a small Starfighter in their Junior range. Mego gained the licence for figure production and brought out a series of nine different small articulated figures on card backing, and a further series of six 12-inch figures in boxes. Mego also produced some of the vehicles, including Buck's Starfighter, a Draconian Marauder ship, a Laserscope fighter (which was not actually in the television show) and a Land Rover vehicle, which is possibly the hardest to find of the Mego *Buck Rogers* toys. A delightful consequence of the new series was that it brought attention to the earlier toys produced relating to *Buck Rogers*. Since the 1920s toys had been made including tinplate spaceships, ray guns and plastic figures, though the early toys are extremely expensive and hard to find.

Early tinplate Marx spaceship from the *Buck Rogers* show. This toy dates back to the 1920s.

Mego large-scale doll of Gil Gerard as Buck in *Buck Rogers in the 25th Century*.

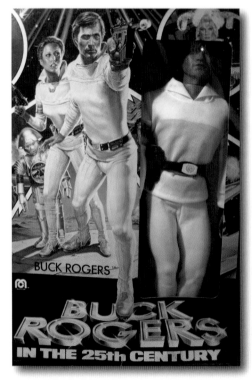

In 1981 Tom Selleck starred in a new series called *Magnum PI*, in which he played a private investigator. Thomas Magnum resided in a guest house on a large estate in Hawaii and lived the high life, driving around in the owner's Ferrari 308 GTS. It was the car that attracted the toy producers, and Corgi brought out a TV-related model car. The car was packaged in a standard Corgi box with a backing card that slots into the box. Without the backing card, the car is a normal Ferrari, so it is the backing card that is highly collectable. Revell Kits also produced a model and LJN Toys manufactured a remote-control red Ferrari with Magnum's image and a plastic figure. The show ran for eight years, but not many collectables were manufactured.

David Hasselhoff sprang to fame in the 1982 programme *Knight Rider*. He played a police officer called Michael Long who was seriously injured in the line of duty; after major surgery and facial reconstruction, he changed his name to Michael Knight and became an agent of Knight Industries. Michael Knight drove a black Pontiac Trans Am called KITT (Knight Industries Two Thousand), which had a computerised brain and the ability to communicate verbally. Again, it was a car that was the star of the show. At the time, very few manufacturers released models of the car. ERTL brought out a small carded version and a larger steel version. Scalextric brought out a race-and-chase set, and a German company, DACDA, released a stunt-car set. Kenner Toys produced an attractive Crash Set featuring the car and the articulated truck in which many of ne scenes were set. They also produced Turbo Booster Car and a Voice Car, oth of which are hard to find.

In 1983 a crack team of Vietnam War veterans appeared in a new series alled *The A-Team*. The four-man Alpha eam comprised Colonel Hannibal Smith George Peppard), Templeton 'Faceman' Peck (Dirk Benedict), B. A. Baracus Mr T) and Howling Mad Murdock Dwight Schulz). The team had been ccused of carrying out a bank robbery n Hanoi and was supposedly on the un from the army authorities. In each pisode, the team helped out someone

Corgi model (298) of a red Ferrari 308GTS as used by Tom Selleck in *Magnum PI.*

n trouble and usually constructed weapons from harmless pieces of garden or arm equipment. Despite the amount of violence and heavy firepower, no one ever appeared to be seriously injured or killed. The A-Team travelled in B. A.'s distinctive black van. Galoob Toys brought out a series of eight figures eaturing the main characters and four villains, all named after snakes (Viper, Rattler, Cobra and Python). They also produced a gift set called 'A-Team Headquarters', which comprised the four figures plus a huge selection of equipment, including guns, rafts, backpacks and radios. There was also a large Command Center set, which comprised a four-storey-high playset for the A-Team. It did not sell in big numbers because of its size. In addition, Galoob brought out a plastic black van set called Tactical Van Playset, which included the figure of B. A. Baracus and a range of equipment inside the van. They also released a plastic armoured car with the figure of Baracus. ERTL Toys produced diecast and steel models of the *A-Team* van as well as Faceman's car, which was a two-tone Corvette sports model. The series ran for nearly five years on British television, with almost one hundred episodes.

In 1983 Gerry Anderson returned to television production with a new show called *Terrahawks*. This was his first puppet show since 1969, though his techniques had now improved vastly. Terrahawks was a secret organisation on Earth which aimed to combat alien invasion. It had

Knight 2000 Crash Set featuring KITT, the computerised car, and the Comtron truck and trailer, manufactured by Kenner Toys.

Galoob carded set
of all four figures
(Colonel Smith,
Face, Mr T
and Mad Dog
Murdock), with
accessories, from
The A-Team.

five human members: Dr 'Tiger' Ninestein, Captain Mary Falconer, Captain Kate Kestrel, Lieutenant Hawkeye and Lieutenant Hiro, who were supported by spherical robots called Zeroids. There was a range of equipment which would make even the Thunderbirds jealous. The main enemy of Earth was Zelda, a Martian android, with her alien allies. The vast majority of collectable toys from this series were produced by the Japanese company Bandai. They made eight carded figures of the main characters and spaceship models in diecast form of the Terrahawks fleet, including the Terrahawk ship, as well as Battlehawk, Treehawk, Spacehawk, Hawkwing and a Battletank.

Later in 1983 London Weekend Television created a new police series called *Dempsey and Makepeace*, which paired a female British police officer Harriet Makepeace (played by Glynis Barber), with a male New York detective called Dempsey (played by Michael Brandon). Their boss at the London

Treehawk
spaceship from the
Gerry Anderson
series *Terrahawks*,
manufactured by
Bandai Toys.

Metropolitan Police was Chief Superintendent Spikings (Ray Smith), who tried to control their unorthodox operations. The show ran for three series in the United Kingdom and was generally popular but never managed to get high ratings in the United States, though it did syndicate well in Europe. Rainbow Toys obtained the merchandising licence and produced a good range of collectable toys. There was a small-scale four-car set consisting of a Ford Escort, Mercedes 500 sports car, Mercedes Benz van and Ford Granada. The cars were also available separately. Rainbow also produced larger-scale models of the Mercedes car with a figure of Dempsey and a Ford Escort car with a figure of Makepeace. There was also a Stunt Race and Chase set, a playset of nine police-related items (handcuffs, whistle, badge and real watch), a carded handcuffs and gun set, and a range of articulated figures of the main characters.

In 1987 a new phenomenon from the United States was launched on British television. *The Teenage Mutant Hero Turtles* were Ninja turtles who lived in the sewers. They were oddly named after famous artists such as Leonardo, Donatello, Michelangelo and Raphael. This popular cartoon series ran for nearly ten years and attracted huge audiences both in Britain and in the United States. Lots of toys were produced, mainly relating to the cartoon characters. Playmates Toys produced the biggest range of figures, including the Turtles, their rat mentor, Splinter, their main enemy, Shredder, and his foot soldiers,

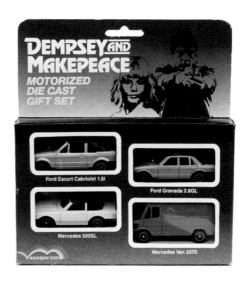

Boxed set of four cars (Ford Escort, Ford Granada, Mercedes 500 SL and Mercedes van) from *Dempsey and Makepeace*, manufactured by Rainbow Toys.

Turtle Blimp and Knucklehead toys, produced by Playmates.

as well as human characters such as April O'Neill and Casey Jones. There were also vehicles such as the Turtles' Party Van, a motorcycle with sidecar, roller-skate vehicle called a Cheapskate, Shredder's car and an airship.

Perhaps the biggest new television series of the 1980s that was to generate TV toy memorabilia was *Star Trek: The Next Generation*. Following on from the 1960s *Star Trek* production, this new show took an entirely new cast and crew for the USS Enterprise and led it in a completely new and updated direction. Starring Patrick Stewart as Captain Jean Luc Picard, and with a full supporting crew, *The Next Generation* was to build on the existing army of 'Trekkies' and to introduce a new fan base. Television filming technology had increased dramatically since the original series, and the special effects, both of the production sets and the alien prosthetics, were much improved. The toy manufacturers loved the new show since it brought opportunities for all kinds of toys – dolls, model kits, costumes, space pistols, diecasts and articulated figures. Books have been written on the subject of *Star Trek* memorabilia, but the main names to look out for are Galoob, AMT, Playmates and Ideal Toys. Galoob issued a set of ten figures for a short period. These included the six main characters from the show as well as four very hard to obtain alien characters (Selay, Anticon, Q and Ferengi). Galoob also released a variety of diecast *Star Trek* ships, as well as accessories such as phaser weapons and communicators. Playmates took over the licence and released a much larger series of figures from the show as well as a large range of plastic ships, both Federation and alien, and accessories. Some of the Playmates models were released as limited editions in smaller numbers, making them more collectable for the diehard *Star Trek* collectors. Ideal Toys produced a wide range of small and affordable models of the *Star Trek* ships and shuttles in a range called 'Micro Machines'. These were made in both small sets and larger sets with limited-edition models.

Large-scale electronic model of the Goddard Shuttlecraft from *Star Trek: The Next Generation*, manufactured by Playmates Toys.

FURTHER READING

BOOKS

Berk, Sally Ann, and Tumbusch, Tom. *Tomart's Encyclopedia of Action Figures*. Black Dog and Leventhal Publishers, 2000.

Berry, Steve. *TV Cream Toys*. The Friday Project, 2007.

Davis, Greg. *Collector's Guide to TV Toys and Memorabilia*. Lister Art Books, 1998.

Davis, Greg, and Morgan, Bill. *Collector's Guide to TV Toys and Memorabilia – 1960s and 1970s*. Collector Books (a division of Schroeder Publishing), 1999.

Force, Ed. *Corgi Toys*. Schiffer Books, 1984.

Force, Ed. *Dinky Toys*. Schiffer Books, 1988.

Marshall, John. *Action Figures of the 1980s*. Schiffer Books, 1998.

Pinsky, Maxine A. *Marx Toys – Robots, Space, Comic, Disney and TB Characters*. Schiffer Books, 1996.

Ramsey, John. *British Diecast Model Toys Catalogue*. Warners Group, 2011.

Stephan, Elizabeth A. *Toy Shop's Action Figure Price Guide*. Krause Publications, 2000.

Tempest, Jack. *Post War Tin Toys – A Collector's Guide*. Eagle Editions, 1998.

Van Cleemput, Marcel R. *The Great Book of Corgi*. New Cavendish Books, 1989.

Ward, Arthur. *TV and Film Toys and Ephemera*. Crowood, 2007.

PERIODICALS

Action Figure Digest. Tomart Publications (bi-monthly).

Collector's Gazette. Warners Group (monthly).

Diecast Collector. Warners Group (monthly).

PLACES TO VISIT

Edinburgh Museum of Childhood, 42 High Street, Royal Mile, Edinburgh EH1 1TG. Telephone: 0131 529 4142. Website: www.edinburghmuseums.org.uk/Venues/Museum-of-Childhood

Hamilton Toy Museum, 111 Main Street, Callander FK17 8BQ. Telephone: 01877 330004. Website: www.thehamiltontoycollection.co.uk

Lothlorien Toy Museum, 22 Well Street, Moffat DG10 9DP. Telephone: 01683 221144. Website: www.lothlorien-emporium.co.uk

Victoria and Albert Museum of Childhood, Cambridge Heath Road, London E2 9PA. Telephone: 020 8983 5200. Website: www.vam.ac.uk/moc

INDEX